EMMANUEL JOSEPH

From Pixels to Power, How Crypto Billionaires Are Building the Countries of Tomorrow

Copyright © 2025 by Emmanuel Joseph

All rights reserved. No part of this publication may be reproduced, stored or transmitted in any form or by any means, electronic, mechanical, photocopying, recording, scanning, or otherwise without written permission from the publisher. It is illegal to copy this book, post it to a website, or distribute it by any other means without permission.

First edition

This book was professionally typeset on Reedsy. Find out more at reedsy.com

Contents

1. Chapter 1: The Birth of Digital Wealth — 1
2. Chapter 2: Reimagining Governance with Blockchain — 3
3. Chapter 3: Building Digital Nations — 5
4. Chapter 4: Decentralized Finance and Economic Transformation — 6
5. Chapter 5: Education and Empowerment through Blockchain — 7
6. Chapter 6: Healthcare Reimagined with Blockchain — 8
7. Chapter 7: Sustainability and Environmental Impact — 9
8. Chapter 8: The Future of Work — 10
9. Chapter 9: Real Estate and Property Ownership — 11
10. Chapter 10: Transport and Mobility — 12
11. Chapter 11: Agriculture and Food Security — 13
12. Chapter 12: Art and Culture in the Digital Age — 14
13. Chapter 13: Travel and Tourism — 16
14. Chapter 14: Urban Planning and Smart Cities — 17
15. Chapter 15: Space Exploration and Colonization — 19
16. Chapter 16: Philanthropy and Social Impact — 21
17. Chapter 17: The Legacy of Crypto Billionaires — 23

1

Chapter 1: The Birth of Digital Wealth

In the dawn of the 21st century, a new form of wealth began to emerge from the nebulous world of bits and bytes. Bitcoin, the pioneering cryptocurrency, transcended the realms of traditional finance, creating a burgeoning ecosystem of digital assets. Unlike conventional currencies, Bitcoin operated on a decentralized, peer-to-peer network, sidestepping the control of central banks and financial institutions. This radical innovation not only democratized finance but also laid the groundwork for a new era of wealth creation.

As Bitcoin's value soared, early adopters and visionary investors reaped substantial rewards. These crypto pioneers, often tech-savvy entrepreneurs, saw their digital fortunes multiply exponentially. The allure of decentralized finance (DeFi) grew stronger, attracting an ever-expanding community of enthusiasts. The rise of Ethereum further propelled this movement, enabling smart contracts and decentralized applications that disrupted traditional industries.

By 2025, the landscape of wealth had fundamentally shifted. Crypto billionaires, with their newfound financial clout, began to explore opportunities beyond the digital realm. These trailblazers envisioned a future where blockchain technology and cryptocurrencies could be harnessed to address global challenges, redefine governance, and reshape economies. The stage was set for an unprecedented transformation, where digital wealth would become a catalyst for building the countries of tomorrow.

2

Chapter 2: Reimagining Governance with Blockchain

Governance has long been plagued by inefficiencies, corruption, and lack of transparency. Enter blockchain technology, with its promise of immutable, decentralized ledgers that could revolutionize how societies are governed. Crypto billionaires, armed with their deep understanding of blockchain, embarked on a mission to reimagine governance systems. They envisioned a future where smart contracts could automate bureaucratic processes, ensuring fairness and accountability.

One of the most ambitious projects was the development of decentralized autonomous organizations (DAOs). These entities operated without centralized control, relying on code to execute decisions based on the consensus of their members. Crypto billionaires invested heavily in DAOs, believing that they could replace traditional government institutions with more efficient, transparent, and democratic alternatives. The success of these initiatives inspired nations to explore blockchain-based governance models, sparking a global movement towards decentralized governance.

Beyond DAOs, blockchain technology was also leveraged to combat corruption. Crypto billionaires funded projects that used blockchain to create tamper-proof records of public transactions, reducing opportunities for fraud and embezzlement. Additionally, blockchain was utilized to ensure the integrity of elections, providing a secure and transparent voting system. These innovations began to restore trust in governance, as citizens witnessed the transformative power of blockchain in action.

3

Chapter 3: Building Digital Nations

The concept of digital nations began to take shape as crypto billionaires sought to create borderless societies governed by blockchain principles. These digital nations, often referred to as "cryptocities," operated independently of traditional nation-states. They offered a unique blend of digital and physical infrastructure, where blockchain technology facilitated everything from governance to economic transactions.

One of the earliest and most prominent cryptocities was BitCity, founded by a consortium of crypto billionaires. BitCity operated on a blockchain-based governance model, with decisions made through decentralized voting and smart contracts. Residents of BitCity enjoyed unprecedented levels of transparency and efficiency, with services such as healthcare, education, and public transportation seamlessly integrated into the blockchain ecosystem.

Crypto billionaires also invested in building sustainable infrastructure for these digital nations. Renewable energy sources powered the cryptocities, and innovative technologies such as vertical farming ensured food security. By leveraging blockchain, they created circular economies that minimized waste and promoted resource efficiency. The success of BitCity inspired the creation of similar digital nations around the world, each with its unique governance model and economic framework.

4

Chapter 4: Decentralized Finance and Economic Transformation

Decentralized finance (DeFi) emerged as a cornerstone of the crypto billionaires' vision for the future. By removing intermediaries, DeFi platforms enabled peer-to-peer financial transactions, lending, and investment, all powered by smart contracts. This democratization of finance provided individuals with greater control over their assets and opened up new opportunities for wealth creation.

Crypto billionaires played a pivotal role in advancing DeFi, investing in innovative platforms that offered a range of financial services. These platforms provided access to loans, savings, and investment opportunities without the need for traditional banks. The transparency and security of blockchain technology instilled confidence in users, leading to widespread adoption of DeFi solutions.

The impact of DeFi extended beyond personal finance, as it began to reshape entire economies. Crypto billionaires collaborated with governments and businesses to integrate DeFi into mainstream financial systems. This integration facilitated cross-border transactions, reduced transaction costs, and promoted financial inclusion. In regions with limited access to traditional banking services, DeFi became a lifeline, empowering individuals and businesses to participate in the global economy.

5

Chapter 5: Education and Empowerment through Blockchain

Education is the foundation of any society, and crypto billionaires recognized the potential of blockchain to revolutionize the learning experience. By leveraging decentralized technology, they aimed to create an inclusive and equitable education system that provided access to quality learning resources for all.

One of the key innovations was the development of blockchain-based educational platforms. These platforms offered a wide range of courses, from basic literacy to advanced technical skills, all accessible through a decentralized network. Students could earn digital certificates and credentials, which were securely stored on the blockchain, ensuring their authenticity and recognition.

Crypto billionaires also invested in initiatives to bridge the digital divide. They funded projects that provided internet access and digital devices to underserved communities, enabling them to participate in the digital economy. By empowering individuals with the knowledge and tools needed to succeed in the modern world, crypto billionaires contributed to building a more inclusive and prosperous future.

6

Chapter 6: Healthcare Reimagined with Blockchain

The healthcare industry has long been plagued by inefficiencies, data breaches, and rising costs. Crypto billionaires saw an opportunity to leverage blockchain technology to address these challenges and create a more efficient and transparent healthcare system.

One of the most significant innovations was the development of blockchain-based health records. These tamper-proof records provided patients with greater control over their data while ensuring its security and privacy. Healthcare providers could access accurate and up-to-date information, leading to better diagnosis and treatment.

Blockchain technology also facilitated the creation of decentralized healthcare platforms. These platforms connected patients with healthcare professionals, enabling remote consultations and telemedicine services. Crypto billionaires invested in these platforms, believing that they could improve access to healthcare, especially in underserved regions.

7

Chapter 7: Sustainability and Environmental Impact

Environmental sustainability was a top priority for crypto billionaires as they built the countries of tomorrow. They recognized the potential of blockchain to promote sustainable practices and reduce the environmental impact of human activities.

One of the key initiatives was the development of blockchain-based supply chain management systems. These systems provided transparency and traceability, enabling consumers to make informed choices about the products they purchased. By promoting ethical and sustainable sourcing, crypto billionaires aimed to reduce the environmental footprint of global supply chains.

Crypto billionaires also invested in renewable energy projects, leveraging blockchain technology to create decentralized energy grids. These grids enabled peer-to-peer energy trading, promoting the use of clean energy sources and reducing reliance on fossil fuels. The success of these initiatives inspired governments and businesses to adopt blockchain-based solutions for sustainability.

8

Chapter 8: The Future of Work

The rise of digital technologies and the gig economy has fundamentally transformed the nature of work. Crypto billionaires recognized the potential of blockchain to further revolutionize the workplace and create new opportunities for individuals and businesses.

One of the key innovations was the development of decentralized job platforms. These platforms connected freelancers and employers, facilitating transparent and secure transactions through smart contracts. Crypto billionaires invested in these platforms, believing that they could create a more equitable and inclusive job market.

Blockchain technology also enabled the creation of decentralized autonomous organizations (DAOs) for the workplace. These DAOs operated without centralized control, allowing employees to participate in decision-making processes and share in the success of the organization. The success of these initiatives inspired businesses to adopt decentralized models, promoting collaboration and innovation.

9

Chapter 9: Real Estate and Property Ownership

The real estate industry has long been plagued by inefficiencies, fraud, and high transaction costs. Crypto billionaires saw an opportunity to leverage blockchain technology to address these challenges and create a more transparent and efficient property market.

One of the key innovations was the development of blockchain-based property registries. These tamper-proof registries provided a secure and transparent record of property ownership, reducing opportunities for fraud and disputes. By promoting trust and transparency, crypto billionaires aimed to create a more efficient property market.

Blockchain technology also facilitated the creation of decentralized real estate platforms. These platforms connected buyers and sellers, enabling transparent and secure transactions through smart contracts. Crypto billionaires invested in these platforms, believing that they could reduce transaction costs and promote financial inclusion in the property market.

10

Chapter 10: Transport and Mobility

The transportation industry has long been plagued by inefficiencies, pollution, and rising costs. Crypto billionaires saw an opportunity to leverage blockchain technology to address these challenges and create a more efficient and sustainable transportation system.

One of the key innovations was the development of blockchain-based mobility platforms. These platforms connected riders and drivers, facilitating transparent and secure transactions through smart contracts. Crypto billionaires invested in these platforms, believing that they could create a more efficient and sustainable transportation system.

Blockchain technology also facilitated the development of decentralized autonomous vehicles (DAVs). These vehicles operated without centralized control, relying on blockchain technology to navigate and communicate with other vehicles. Crypto billionaires invested in these vehicles, believing that they could reduce traffic congestion and promote sustainable mobility.

11

Chapter 11: Agriculture and Food Security

The agriculture industry, essential for human survival, faced issues like inefficiencies, fraud, and food insecurity. Crypto billionaires identified blockchain technology as a solution to these challenges, aiming to create a more transparent and efficient food system.

One significant innovation was blockchain-based supply chain management systems for agriculture. These systems offered transparency and traceability from farm to table, ensuring the authenticity and safety of food products. Consumers could verify the origins of their food, fostering trust and promoting sustainable agricultural practices.

Blockchain also facilitated the creation of decentralized agricultural platforms. These platforms connected farmers with buyers, enabling transparent and secure transactions through smart contracts. Crypto billionaires invested in these platforms, believing that they could reduce transaction costs and promote financial inclusion for small-scale farmers.

Additionally, blockchain technology enabled the development of decentralized food security networks. These networks utilized smart contracts to automate the distribution of food aid, ensuring that it reached those in need. Crypto billionaires funded these initiatives, aiming to combat hunger and promote food security on a global scale.

12

Chapter 12: Art and Culture in the Digital Age

The world of art and culture experienced a paradigm shift with the advent of blockchain technology. Crypto billionaires recognized the potential of blockchain to revolutionize the creative industries, providing artists and creators with new opportunities to monetize their work.

One of the most significant innovations was the development of blockchain-based platforms for art and digital assets. These platforms enabled artists to tokenize their creations, turning them into unique, verifiable digital assets known as non-fungible tokens (NFTs). Crypto billionaires invested in these platforms, believing that they could empower artists and creators to retain control over their work and earn fair compensation.

Blockchain technology also facilitated the creation of decentralized marketplaces for art and digital assets. These marketplaces provided a secure and transparent environment for buying, selling, and trading NFTs. Crypto billionaires supported these initiatives, believing that they could democratize access to art and culture, making it more inclusive and accessible to a global audience.

Beyond the visual arts, blockchain technology also impacted other creative industries, such as music and literature. Decentralized platforms enabled artists and writers to publish their work directly to their audiences, bypassing traditional intermediaries. This new model promoted creative freedom and ensured that artists received fair compensation for their work.

13

Chapter 13: Travel and Tourism

The travel and tourism industry, a vital component of the global economy, faced numerous challenges, including fraud, inefficiencies, and high transaction costs. Crypto billionaires saw an opportunity to leverage blockchain technology to address these issues and create a more transparent and efficient travel ecosystem.

One of the key innovations was the development of blockchain-based travel platforms. These platforms connected travelers with service providers, facilitating transparent and secure transactions through smart contracts. Crypto billionaires invested in these platforms, believing that they could create a more efficient and enjoyable travel experience for everyone.

Blockchain technology also enabled the development of decentralized travel networks. These networks utilized smart contracts to automate various aspects of travel, such as booking accommodations, purchasing tickets, and accessing services. Crypto billionaires supported these initiatives, believing that they could reduce transaction costs and promote financial inclusion in the travel industry.

Additionally, blockchain technology facilitated the creation of decentralized loyalty programs for travelers. These programs used blockchain to reward travelers with tokens that could be redeemed for various services and experiences. Crypto billionaires invested in these programs, aiming to promote customer loyalty and enhance the overall travel experience.

14

Chapter 14: Urban Planning and Smart Cities

The rapid growth of urban populations presented numerous challenges, including congestion, pollution, and inefficiencies. Crypto billionaires recognized the potential of blockchain technology to address these issues and create more sustainable and efficient cities.

One of the key innovations was the development of blockchain-based urban planning platforms. These platforms utilized blockchain to collect and analyze data on various aspects of urban life, such as traffic, energy consumption, and waste management. Crypto billionaires invested in these platforms, believing that they could create more efficient and sustainable urban environments.

Blockchain technology also facilitated the development of smart city initiatives. These initiatives used blockchain to integrate various urban systems, such as transportation, utilities, and public services, into a seamless and efficient network. Crypto billionaires supported these initiatives, believing that they could create more livable and sustainable cities.

Additionally, blockchain technology enabled the creation of decentralized urban governance models. These models utilized smart contracts to automate various aspects of city management, such as resource allocation and service delivery. Crypto billionaires invested in these models, aiming to create more transparent and accountable urban governance systems.

15

Chapter 15: Space Exploration and Colonization

The final frontier of space exploration and colonization presented new opportunities for crypto billionaires to leverage blockchain technology. They envisioned a future where blockchain could facilitate the development of space industries and the creation of off-Earth colonies.

One of the key innovations was the development of blockchain-based space exploration platforms. These platforms utilized blockchain to coordinate and manage various aspects of space missions, such as resource allocation, communication, and navigation. Crypto billionaires invested in these platforms, believing that they could create more efficient and sustainable space missions.

Blockchain technology also facilitated the development of decentralized space industries. These industries utilized blockchain to create transparent and secure supply chains for space resources, such as minerals and fuel. Crypto billionaires supported these initiatives, believing that they could promote the growth of space economies and reduce reliance on Earth-based resources.

Additionally, blockchain technology enabled the creation of decentralized governance models for off-Earth colonies. These models utilized smart contracts to automate various aspects of colony management, such as resource allocation and conflict resolution. Crypto billionaires invested in these models, aiming to create more transparent and accountable governance systems for space colonies.

16

Chapter 16: Philanthropy and Social Impact

Crypto billionaires recognized the potential of blockchain technology to address social challenges and promote philanthropy. They envisioned a future where blockchain could facilitate the distribution of aid, promote transparency, and ensure that resources reached those in need.

One of the key innovations was the development of blockchain-based philanthropy platforms. These platforms utilized blockchain to create transparent and secure records of donations and aid distribution. Crypto billionaires invested in these platforms, believing that they could promote trust and accountability in philanthropy.

Blockchain technology also facilitated the development of decentralized social impact networks. These networks utilized smart contracts to automate the distribution of resources and services to underserved communities. Crypto billionaires supported these initiatives, believing that they could promote financial inclusion and reduce inequality.

Additionally, blockchain technology enabled the creation of impact tokens, which represented shares in social impact projects. These tokens allowed individuals and organizations to invest in projects that aligned with their values, promoting a new model of socially responsible investing. Crypto billionaires invested in these tokens, aiming to create a more sustainable and equitable world.

17

Chapter 17: The Legacy of Crypto Billionaires

As the crypto billionaires continued to build the countries of tomorrow, their legacy began to take shape. They had leveraged blockchain technology to address global challenges, promote transparency, and create more inclusive and equitable societies.

Their vision of a decentralized future had inspired governments, businesses, and individuals to embrace blockchain technology and explore its potential. The impact of their work could be seen in various sectors, from finance and governance to education and healthcare.

The crypto billionaires' legacy was not just about the wealth they had accumulated but also about the positive change they had brought to the world. Their innovative solutions had empowered individuals, promoted sustainability, and created new opportunities for growth and development.

As the world continued to evolve, the influence of crypto billionaires would be felt for generations to come. Their vision of a decentralized, transparent, and inclusive future had set the stage for a new era of progress and prosperity, where the power of technology was harnessed to build a better world for all.

From Pixels to Power: How Crypto Billionaires Are Building the Countries of Tomorrow

In the digital age, the rise of cryptocurrencies has not only created immense wealth but also sparked a revolutionary movement towards decentralized governance, finance, and innovation. "From Pixels to Power" delves into the transformative journey of crypto billionaires who are leveraging blockchain technology to build the countries of tomorrow.

This book explores the visionary efforts of these pioneers as they reimagine governance, create sustainable infrastructure, and promote financial inclusion. From decentralized autonomous organizations (DAOs) to digital nations and blockchain-based supply chain management, crypto billionaires are pushing the boundaries of what's possible.

Discover how these trailblazers are using decentralized finance (DeFi) to reshape economies, revolutionize education, and transform healthcare. Learn about their initiatives to promote sustainability, empower underserved communities, and create a more transparent and accountable world.

Through captivating stories and insightful analysis, "From Pixels to Power" sheds light on the impact of crypto billionaires and their quest to build a better future. This book is a testament to the power of innovation, collaboration, and the relentless pursuit of progress in the digital era.

www.ingramcontent.com/pod-product-compliance
Lightning Source LLC
LaVergne TN
LVHW020743090526
838202LV00057BA/6202